ETFs Explained

The Ultimate Guide to Exchange-Traded Funds

Robert M. Watson

Disclaimer

The information provided in this book is for general informational purposes only and is not intended to be, and should not be taken as, financial, investment, or legal advice. The author and publisher of this book are not financial advisors and do not endorse or recommend any particular investment or financial strategy.

Investing involves risk, including the risk of loss. The value of your investments may fluctuate and you may lose money. Past performance is not indicative of future results. It is important to carefully consider your financial goals, risk tolerance, and other personal factors before making any investment decisions.

You should consult with a financial professional before making any investment decisions and carefully review a l relevant documents, including prospectuses, before investing. The author and publisher of this book are not responsible for any errors or omissions, or for any actions taken based on the information contained in this book.

This book is not a substitute for professional financial advice and should not be relied upon as such. The author and publisher of this book do not guarantee the accuracy, completeness, or usefulness of the information contained in this book and will not be liable for any errors or omissions, or for any actions taken based on the information contained in this book.

Contents

Chapter 1: Introduction to ETFs

1.1 What are ETFs? Basic Definition and Overview of ETFs

Pull up a chair and pour yourself a glass of your favorite beverage – whether it's a cup of tea, a nice glass of scotch, or even a mug of hot cocoa (don't worry, we won't judge!). Because we're about to journey into the captivating world of ETFs. Now, you might be thinking: what on earth is an ETF? Is it some sort of alien technology? Well, sorry to disappoint you, my dear UFO enthusiasts, but ETFs have less to do with extraterrestrial life and more to do with down-to-earth investing.

Picture yourself at a buffet, the kind with more food options than your grandmother's Thanksgiving feast. You've got the prime rib, the seafood, the roasted vegetables, and oh, let's not forget about the delectable desserts. That's what an ETF (Exchange-Traded Fund) is like, but for investments.

An ETF is a type of security that involves a collection of securities—such as stocks—that often tracks an underlying index. In our buffet analogy, the "underlying index" is the menu and the "collection of securities" are the tantalizingly diverse dishes you can pile onto your plate. Some ETFs don't track an index, much like those rogue buffet attendees who ignore the menu and just pile on the lobster tails (we see you!). These ETFs are structured to follow certain investment strategies.

ETFs are similar to mutual funds, but there's a key difference. While mutual funds are a bit like a members-only club that only lets you in or out once a day at the day's closing price, ETFs are more democratic. They're traded on exchanges just like individual stocks and can be bought and sold throughout the trading day at prices that change based on supply and demand. You can buy just one share of an ETF or you can buy a million, assuming you have the cash (if you do, can we be friends?).

So in essence, ETFs offer you a way to invest in a diverse selection of assets without needing to buy each one individually. It's a one-stop shop for diversification – like Amazon, but for stocks, bonds, or even commodities.

While the concept of ETFs might seem as perplexing as the Bermuda Triangle, it's actually a straightforward and efficient investment vehicle once you get the hang of it. So strap in, because we're about to demystify the enigmatic ETF and guide you through the ins and outs of these investment powerhouses. Stay tuned for more delectable investment insights and borderline sensible analogies!

1.2 History of ETFs: The Origin and Evolution of ETFs

In the mood for a little story time? Gather round the financial campfire, dear readers, as we venture into the annals of investment history, a journey packed with innovation, monetary maneuvering, and yes, more food analogies. Our story begins in the funky times of the early 1990s, when shoulder pads were all the rage and the internet was just a baby.

A Product of the '90s

Way back in 1993, the first ETF was born in the U.S., a time when 'Friends' was just a flicker on NBC's drawing board. This ETF was called the Standard & Poor's Depository Receipts (SPDR), but you may know it by its catchy nickname, "Spider" (not to be confused with Spiderman). The Spider was, and still is, designed to track the S&P 500 Index, meaning it's a smorgasbord of 500 of the largest U.S. companies.

The ETF Boom

The Spider proved to be more than just a web in the investment world. Seeing the success of the Spider ETF, other investment companies began to launch their own versions of ETFs. And thus, the 2000s witnessed an ETF boom, much like the dotcom boom, but with fewer GeoCities pages and more portfolios.

This was the period that gave birth to a broad spectrum of ETFs. There were ETFs tracking the whole U.S. stock market, such as the Vanguard Total Stock Market ETF. Then there were sector-specific ETFs, like the Financial Select Sector SPDR Fund. International ETFs also began to make their appearance, offering investors exposure to foreign markets without the need for a passport or jet lag.

And it wasn't just equities getting the ETF treatment. Bonds joined the ETF party, too. In 2002, iShares launched the first bond ETF, making it easier for individual investors to gain exposure to the bond market. Prior to this, investing in individual bonds was like trying to find a needle in a haystack. With bond ETFs, investors could gain broad exposure to the bond market with the purchase of a single ETF.

12

Innovations and Variations

From there, the ETF world has only continued to expand and evolve, like a universe in a never-ending state of financial inflation. Nowadays, we have commodity ETFs that track the price of everything from gold to oil. There are thematic ETFs that focus on specific trends or sectors, such as renewable energy or technology. We even have leveraged and inverse ETFs that aim to return the multiple or the inverse of their benchmark.

And thus, my friends, we find ourselves in the current age, where the ETF universe is as diverse as a New York City food festival. From humble beginnings as a single spider web, the ETF world has expanded into a vast, diverse ecosystem, offering something for every kind of investor. Whether you're a conservative retiree or a risk-taking young gun, there's likely an ETF out there with your name on it.

There you have it, a stroll down the memory lane of ETFs. But buckle up, the journey has just begun. Up next, we dive into the mechanics of ETFs and explain how these mysterious creatures actually work. Spoiler alert: it involves more than just magic and pixie dust.

1.3 Types of ETFs: Descriptions of the Main Types of ETFs

Now that we've toured the illustrious history of ETFs, let's delve into the meat and potatoes of the matter: the different types of ETFs. Strap on your investment safari hats, as we're about to embark on a whirlwind tour of the wild ETF landscape, where we'll encounter a variety of species, each with its own unique characteristics and behaviors.

Index ETFs: The Backbone of the ETF World

First up, we have the Index ETFs, the granddaddies of them all. These guys aim to track specific indexes, like the S&P 500 or the Dow Jones Industrial Average. They're a bit like a cover band: they try their best to mimic the performance of the original, be it the Beatles or the FTSE 100. So, if you ever want to invest in the entire U.S. stock market with just one purchase, this is your ticket!

Sector ETFs: The Specialists

Next, we encounter the Sector ETFs. They're the specialists of the ETF world. They focus on a specific industry or sector such as technology, healthcare, or finance. Consider these guys like your food delivery app: If you've got a hankering for pizza, you don't order a smorgasbord of every cuisine. You zero in on the pizza joints. Similarly, if you believe the technology sector will outperform, you might want to order up a Sector ETF that focuses on tech stocks.

Commodity ETFs: The Tangibles

Continuing our safari, we come across the Commodity ETFs, the hard assets of the ETF universe. These ETFs invest in commodities like gold, oil, or even corn. So if you've ever wanted to own a barrel of oil without, you know, actually owning a barrel of oil, these are for you. They're the digital equivalent of old-school treasure chests filled with tangible riches.

Bond ETFs: The Loan Rangers

Now, we move onto the Bond ETFs, also known as the loan rangers. Instead of stocks or commodities, they invest in bonds, essentially loaning money to governments or companies in return for regular interest payments. If equities are the wild, roller-coaster-riding thrill-seekers of the investment world, bond ETFs are the calm, teacup-ride enthusiasts. They typically offer more stability, but with lower potential returns.

International ETFs: The Globetrotters

And last, but certainly not least, we have the International ETFs, the globetrotters of the ETF landscape. These ETFs offer exposure to markets outside of your home country. Whether it's the emerging markets of India and China or the developed markets of Europe and Japan, International ETFs allow you to see the world without leaving your couch or quarantining for two weeks.

From the broad-reaching Index ETFs to the niche Sector ETFs, the physical Commodity ETFs to the predictable Bond ETFs, and the adventurous International ETFs, the ETF world is as rich and diverse as a well-stocked cheese board. Each type of ETF serves a different purpose and fits into your portfolio in its own unique way, just like a jigsaw puzzle piece. Up next, we'll explore how to fit these pieces together to create a beautiful investing picture. Stay tuned!

1.4 Why ETFs? Benefits and Drawbacks of Investing in ETFs

In our grand saga of the ETF universe, we've now reached the critical chapter that tackles the quintessential question: why ETFs? What makes them the belle of the investment ball? And are they truly as perfect as your grandma's apple pie, or do they come with a side of financial heartburn? Hold on to your hats, folks, as we're about to embark on a roller coaster ride of pros and cons.

The Winsome Benefits of ETFs

Diversification: The Spices of Life

In the realm of investing, diversification is the magical cloak that shields you from excessive risk. ETFs, with their 'all-you-can-invest' approach, offer a convenient path to diversification. Instead of buying shares in a single company and putting all your eggs in one basket (a basket that could very well topple over), you get a little slice of many pies. And who doesn't love more pie?

Flexibility: The Stretchy Pants of Investing

Remember our distinction between mutual funds and ETFs? ETFs trade like individual stocks, meaning you can buy and sell them throughout the trading day at market prices. You're not locked into an end-of-day price like with mutual funds. It's like stretchy pants at Thanksgiving – you get all the room you need to make your moves.

Lower Costs: The Dollar Menu of the Finance World

Many ETFs have lower expense ratios than mutual funds, which makes them the financially savvy choice for the cost-conscious investor. It's like getting a gourmet meal for the price of fast food. More bang for your buck, as they say.

The Not-So-Sunny Side of ETFs

While ETFs seem like the golden child of the investment world, it's important to remember that all that glitters is not gold. There are, of course, a few potential pitfalls to be wary of when venturing into ETF territory.

Liquidity Traps: The Slow Dance of the Market

While most ETFs have high liquidity (i.e., they can be easily bought and sold), not all ETFs are created equal. Some niche ETFs might not be as popular, leading to low trading volumes and wider bid-ask spreads. It's like being the last one on the dance floor – not always a comfortable position to be in.

Leveraged and Inverse ETFs: The High-Stakes Casino

While traditional ETFs can be a relatively safe bet, the same cannot be said for all types. Leveraged and inverse ETFs can be extremely risky and are more akin to gambling than investing. These exotic ETFs might sound intriguing, but tread carefully, dear readers. High risk can lead to high rewards, but also to dramatic losses.

ETFs, like everything else in life (including grandma's apple pie), come with both advantages and pitfalls. But with a bit of knowledge and careful navigation, they can be a powerful tool in your investment toolbox. Up next, we'll be diving deeper into the fascinating world of ETFs, providing you with the roadmap you need to navigate this thrilling terrain. Stay tuned!

Chapter 2: Understanding ETF Mechanics

2.1 How ETFs Work: Structure and Operation of ETFs

It's time to pop the hood and take a gander at the engine that powers our ETF machine. Yes, we're about to delve into the exciting world of ETF mechanics. If you're expecting spark plugs and oil changes, you might be slightly disappointed. But fear not! We promise this won't be a snoozefest akin to reading an appliance manual. Instead, we'll dive into the nitty-gritty, the gears and gizmos, of how ETFs work.

The Structure: The Bare Bones

As we've learned, an ETF is a basket of securities that you can buy or sell through a brokerage firm on a stock exchange. But here's the fun part: ETFs are structured in such a way that the fund's ownership of the actual assets is separated from the ownership of the ETF shares themselves.

The asset manager (the company that sets up the ETF) works with a group of financial institutions, called Authorized Participants (APs), who have the superpower to create or redeem ETF shares. These APs are typically large institutional organizations, such as Bank of America or Goldman Sachs, not your next-door neighbor Jim who's really good at fixing bicycles.

The Operation: The Dance of Creation and Redemption

Now let's take a peek at the creation and redemption process – the secret sauce of ETFs operation.

Creation

The birth of an ETF unit starts with the asset manager setting up an agreement with the AP. The asset manager outlines the recipe for the ETF, i.e., the list of securities in the desired proportions. Then, the AP goes shopping! They purchase all the necessary securities and hands them over to the asset manager. In return, the asset manager gives the AP a proportionate number of new ETF shares. Voila! An ETF unit is born.

Redemption

The redemption process is basically the creation process in reverse. If an AP wants to get rid of their ETF shares (maybe they're Marie Kondo-ing their portfolio), they give the shares back to the asset manager. In return, the asset manager gives them the equivalent value in the ETF's underlying securities. The ETF shares are effectively 'destroyed', and the AP can then sell those individual securities on the open market.

The Intricacies: The Need-to-Know Nuances

This constant dance of creation and redemption helps keep an ETF's market price close to its net asset value (NAV), which is the total market value of all the securities held by the ETF divided by the number of ETF shares. Essentially, it's what each share of the ETF should be worth based on its assets. If the price of an ETF starts to drift away from its NAV, the APs can step in and arbitrage the difference, creating or redeeming shares to bring the price back in line.

One last tidbit: unlike mutual funds, individual investors typically cannot directly buy into or redeem out of the fund's holdings. You can only buy or sell ETF shares on the open market. But don't fret – that's why we have APs to do the heavy lifting!

And there you have it, the basic mechanics of an ETF! It's a bit like a well-choreographed ballet, with each participant knowing their role and when to make their move. Up next, we'll dive into the strategies you can employ to get these dancers moving to your tune. Stay tuned!

2.2 Pricing and Liquidity: Understanding How ETFs Are Priced and Their Liquidity

Ready for another round of investment wisdom? Brace yourselves because we're about to dive into the exciting world of pricing and liquidity. Now, I know what you're thinking. "Exciting? Really?" Bear with me. It's like finding a perfectly ripe avocado at the supermarket: maybe not Hollywood blockbuster thrilling, but still a small victory in its own right. Let's get to it!

ETF Pricing: The Price Is Right (Mostly)

When it comes to pricing, ETFs are somewhat like a chameleon. Throughout the day, they change their color (price) to match their surroundings (the value of their underlying assets). The price of an ETF is determined by the tug-of-war between buyers and sellers throughout the trading day, much like individual stocks.

But unlike stocks, ETFs have a secret weapon that helps keep their price in line with the value of their underlying assets. This weapon is the Net Asset Value (NAV), the per-share value of all the securities held in the ETF. The NAV is calculated at the end of the trading day, and it's like the North Star for ETFs, providing a guiding light towards what the ETF's price should be.

But what happens when the price and the NAV aren't in sync? That's where our superhero Authorized Participants (APs) come in. Remember them from our previous discussion on ETF mechanics? If the ETF's price starts to deviate significantly from its NAV, APs swoop in to perform an arbtrage operation, which helps nudge the ETF price back towards its NAV.

Liquidity: Keep the Cash Flowing

Liquidity refers to how easy it is to buy or sell something without affecting its price. If you've ever tried to sell your collection of vintage Beanie Babies, only to find no interested buyers, you've experienced low liquidity.

In the world of ETFs, liquidity is a bit of a complex beast. It's affected by two things: the liquidity of the ETF shares themselves and the liquidity of the ETF's underlying assets.

The first one is straightforward. ETF shares are bought and sold on exchanges just like stocks. The more active the trading, the more liquid the ETF is considered to be. A highly traded ETF like the SPDR S&P 500 ETF (SPY) will have high liquidity, while a niche ETF with few buyers and sellers may be less liquid.

But the plot thickens! Even if an ETF isn't heavily traded, it can still have good liquidity if its underlying assets are liquid. Remember our Authorized Participants? If there's a big demand for an ETF, an AP can simply create more shares, and if demand drops, they can redeem shares, both of which can help keep the ETF's price in line with its NAV.

Understanding the pricing and liquidity of ETFs is an essential part of your investing journey. Like finding the perfectly ripe avocado, it may take a little bit of knowledge and a bit of practice, but the results are definitely worth it. In our next section, we'll dive into the various ways you can slice and dice those avocados (i.e., use ETFs in your investment strategies). Stay tuned!

2.3 Creation and Redemption Process

The ETF Creation/Redemption Process Explained

We've reached the part in our ETF journey where we'll watch the miracle of life and the inevitability of death play out in the financial market. Don't worry; it's not as grim as it sounds! We're simply talking about the life cycle of an ETF unit, also known as the creation and redemption process. Now, gather around, folks, as we witness the magic that keeps the ETF market humming along smoothly.

Creation: The Miracle of ETF Birth

The birth of an ETF share starts with the fund manager, who publishes a shopping list, known as the "creation basket". This list contains all the securities that make up the ETF. And who's in charge of the shopping? Our trusty Authorized Participants (APs), of course!

The AP scoops up all the securities on the list in the right proportions, essentially putting together a perfect mini version of the ETF. Once they've got everything in their cart, they bring it to the fund manager. In return, the fund manager gives the AP a bundle of fresh, newly created ETF shares. The AP can then sell these shares on the stock market to investors like you and me.

This whole process is known as "in-kind" creation because the fund manager is swapping securities for ETF shares, rather than transacting in cold, hard cash. This method has its perks, like keeping the fund's trading costs low and helping it avoid triggering capital gains taxes.

Redemption: The Circle of ETF Life

Redemption is the other side of this cycle, and it's just the creation process in reverse. When an AP wants to get rid of their ETF shares, they bring them back to the fund manager, who swaps them for a batch of the ETF's underlying securities. This bundle of securities, known as the "redemption basket", is essentially a mirror image of the creation basket.

And what happens to those ETF shares? Well, just like a retired Vegas magician's disappearing trick, they vanish! The AP takes the securities and sells them on the market.

Balancing Act: The Great Equalizer

This back-and-forth process serves as a balancing mechanism for the ETF's market price. If the ETF's price starts to drift too far from the value of its underlying assets (its net asset value, or NAV), our APs can swoop in to take advantage of this discrepancy and bring the prices back in line. It's like a financial see-saw that always tries to find its equilibrium.

And there you have it! The life and death (or creation and redemption) of an ETF share. It's a bit of financial wizardry, but it's the magic that keeps the ETF market fair, balanced, and efficient. Up next, we're strapping on our tool belts and looking at how to use ETFs in your investment strategy.

2.4 ETFs vs. Mutual Funds: Differences and Similarities Between ETFs and Mutual Funds

It's time for the showdown you've all been waiting for. In the blue corner, we have the nimble, versatile newcomer, the ETF! And in the red corner, the established, steady heavyweight, the mutual fund! This is going to be a no-holds-barred, toe-to-toe clash of investment titans. Okay, maybe it's not as dramatic as all that, but it's important to understand how these two investment vehicles stack up against each other.

Similarities: Birds of a Feather

Before we get into the rumble, let's start with a group hug. ETFs and mutual funds are similar in many ways. Both are investment funds that allow you to buy a diversified pool of securities in one fell swoop. They're both overseen by professional money managers and are a great way to gain exposure to a broad range of assets without having to buy each one individually. Kind of like buying a party mix instead of individual snacks.

Differences: Clash of the Titans

But let's get to the good stuff: the differences! There are several key distinctions between ETFs and mutual funds, and we'll break them down blow by blow.

Round 1: Trading Flexibility

Here's where ETFs throw the first punch. Unlike mutual funds, which are only priced and traded at the end of the trading day, ETFs can be bought and sold throughout the day like stocks. This allows for more flexibility and the opportunity to react quickly to market changes.

Round 2: Minimum Investments

Mutual funds strike back in this round. Many mutual funds require a minimum investment, which can range from a few hundred to several thousand dollars. On the other hand, with ETFs, there is no minimum investment beyond the cost of one share. This makes ETFs more accessible to investors with smaller portfolios.

Round 3: Expense Ratios

ETFs land another hit here. ETFs generally have lower expense ratios than mutual funds, making them a more cost-effective choice for many investors. But remember, not all ETFs and mutual funds are created equal, so always check the fine print!

Round 4: Tax Efficiency

Thanks to the "in-kind" creation and redemption process we discussed earlier, ETFs are generally more tax-efficient than mutual funds. This is because the in-kind process allows ETFs to avoid triggering capital gains taxes that could be passed on to the investor.

Round 5: Dividends

This one's a bit of a draw. Both ETFs and mutual funds can offer dividends to their investors. However, mutual funds typically reinvest dividends immediately, while ETFs accumulate the dividends and pay them out to shareholders on a periodic basis.

As you can see, both ETFs and mutual funds have their strengths and weaknesses. The key is understanding these differences so you can pick the right contender for your investment portfolio. Stay tuned for the next chapter where we'll talk strategies to make ETFs work for your financial goals.

Chapter 3: Diving into Index ETFs

3.1 Understanding Indexes: Overview of Market Indexes

Roll up your sleeves, because we're about to dig into the foundation that underpins many ETFs: market indexes. If you're picturing a guy in a green visor scribbling in a ledger, you're in for a surprise! The world of indexes is more akin to a high-speed train, chugging along, constantly recalibrating its route as it carries investors on the journey toward potential profits. Let's dive in!

Indexes 101: What's an Index, Anyway?

At its heart, a market index is simply a method of tracking the performance of a specific group of securities. Think of it as the financial world's version of a mixtape (or playlist, for the younger folks out there). But instead of compiling your favorite 80s hits, a market index compiles a group of securities that represent a particular segment of the market.

For example, the S&P 500 Index is a popular US index that tracks the performance of 500 of the largest publicly traded companies in the country. It's a pretty reliable snapshot of the US large-cap market. Just like you might judge the state of 80s music by the songs on your mixtape, investors look at the S&P 500 to gauge how the US large-cap market is doing.

The Inner Workings: How are Indexes Calculated?

The way an index is calculated can be quite simple or really complicated, depending on the index. Some indexes, like the Dow Jones Industrial Average, are price-weighted, which means companies with higher stock prices have a greater influence on the index's value.

Others, like our friend the S&P 500, are market-cap weighted. That means companies with larger market capitalizations (the total market value of a company's outstanding shares of stock) have a more significant impact on the index's value.

Then there are equal-weighted indexes, fundamentally weighted indexes, and more. It's like making a mixtape based on song length, artist popularity, or the singer's hair volume (if we're sticking with the 80s theme). Each method gives a slightly different perspective on the market.

Indexes and ETFs: A Match Made in Heaven

Many ETFs are designed to track a specific market index, earning them the name "index ETFs". The goal of an index ETF is to mimic the performance of its underlying index as closely as possible. How? By holding the same securities in the same proportions as the index.

For instance, an S&P 500 ETF will hold the same 500 companies that the S&P 500 Index does. If you invest in this ETF, you're essentially investing in a tiny piece of those 500 companies. It's like buying the entire 80s mixtape instead of trying to acquire each song individually. Much easier, right?

So there you have it! Indexes, in a nutshell. They're a vital part of understanding how ETFs work and why they're a handy tool for investors. Up next, we'll delve deeper into the world of index ETFs, and explore how they can be a powerful part of your investment strategy.

3.2 Index ETFs Explained: In-Depth Explanation of Index ETFs

What's an Index ETF, Anyway?

In the simplest terms, an index ETF is a fund that aims to mimic the performance of a specific market index, like the S&P 500 or the Dow Jones Industrial Average. Remember our mixtape analogy from before? If an index is a mixtape, an index ETF is like a band covering all the songs on that mixtape. The band's goal is to reproduce the songs as faithfully as possible, and an index ETF aims to reproduce the performance of its underlying index as closely as it can.

The Fine Art of Replication

Index ETFs replicate the performance of their underlying index by holding the same securities, in the same proportions. For example, an index ETF tracking the S&P 500 will hold all 500 companies included in that index, in proportion to their market capitalizations.

However, sometimes a faithful replication isn't possible or practical, especially for indexes that track a large number of securities or hard-to-reach markets. In these cases, an index ETF might use a technique called sampling, where it holds a representative selection of securities from the index. It's like a cover band that can't afford a full orchestra, so they use a synthesizer instead. It's not exactly the same, but it can still sound pretty good!

Benefits of Index ETFs: The Good Stuff

Index ETFs have several features that make them attractive to investors. Here are some of the highlights:

Diversification: Buying an index ETF is like getting a sampler platter of the market. You get exposure to a wide range of companies, sectors, or asset classes, all in one package.

Cost-efficiency: Because they're passively managed (i.e., they simply follow an index rather than making active investment decisions), index ETFs usually have lower expense ratios than actively managed funds.

Transparency: ETFs disclose their holdings daily, so you always know what you're invested in.

Flexibility: Like all ETFs, index ETFs can be bought and sold throughout the trading day at market prices.

The Catch: Potential Drawbacks

As great as index ETFs can be, they're not without their quirks. Here are a couple of things to keep in mind:

Market-cap bias: Market-cap-weighted index ETFs are biased towards larger companies, which can lead to over-concentration in certain sectors or companies.

Lack of active management: Since index ETFs are passively managed, they won't make defensive moves in response to market conditions. If the market goes down, your index ETF will go down with it.

Like any investment, they have their pros and cons, but understanding how they work can help you decide if they're right for your portfolio. Up next, we'll explore the different flavors of index ETFs, from broad market to sector to international ETFs.

3.3 Popular Index ETFs: Examples and Their Features

It's time to take a tour of the index ETF aquarium, where we'll showcase some of the most popular index ETFs swimming in the investment waters. Strap on your snorkel, because here we go!

The Broad-Market Titans

These are the index ETFs that try to cover as much of the market as they can. They're like the whale sharks of the ETF world - big, slow, and steady.

SPDR S&P 500 ETF (SPY): The granddaddy of all ETFs, the SPY aims to replicate the performance of the S&P 500 Index. It's the most traded ETF in the world and gives investors exposure to a broad swathe of the U.S. large-cap market.

Vanguard Total Stock Market ETF (VTI): The VTI is like a one-stop-shop for U.S. stocks. It seeks to track the performance of the CRSP US Total Market Index, which includes large-, mid-, and small-cap stocks. It's a more diversified option than the SPY, as it includes smaller companies in its mix.

The Sector Surfers

These ETFs focus on specific sectors of the market. They're like the dolphins of the ETF world - quick, agile, and perfect for riding the waves of sector trends.

Technology Select Sector SPDR Fund (XLK): The XLK gives investors exposure to the tech sector of the S&P 500. It's heavy on companies like Apple and Microsoft and is a popular choice for investors looking to ride the tech wave.

Health Care Select Sector SPDR Fund (XLV): The XLV tracks the healthcare sector of the S&P 500. It includes pharmaceutical giants, biotech innovators, and healthcare service providers.

The International Explorers

These ETFs give investors exposure to markets outside the U.S. They're like the sea turtles of the ETF world - always ready for a long-distance journey.

iShares MSCI EAFE ETF (EFA): The EFA gives investors exposure to stocks in developed markets outside of the U.S. and Canada. EFA is a good choice for diversifying your portfolio internationally.

Vanguard FTSE Emerging Markets ETF (VWO): The VWO tracks an index that includes stocks from emerging markets like China, India, and Brazil. It's a higher-risk, higher-reward option for those looking to add some international spice to their portfolio.

A VIP tour of the index ETF aquarium. Remember, these are just a few examples, and there are many more index ETFs out there, each with its own unique features and quirks. The important thing is to find the ones that fit your investment goals and risk tolerance.

3.4 Investing in Index ETFs: Strategies for Riding the Index ETF Wave

The Buy-and-Hold Behemoth

The most common strategy for investing in index ETFs is the buy-and-hold approach. It's like the blue whale of strategies - slow-moving, but with the power to cover great distances over time. With this strategy, you buy index ETFs and hold onto them for a long period, allowing the market to do its thing.

The key to this approach is patience and consistency. It's like being a marathon swimmer in the investment ocean; it's not about sprinting to the finish line but enduring the long journey.

Remember, though, that even a buy-and-hold strategy should involve regular reviews of your portfolio to ensure it aligns with your financial goals and risk tolerance.

The Sector-Specific Shark

If the buy-and-hold strategy is like a blue whale, the sector-specific strategy is more like a shark, swift and focused. This strategy involves investing in sector-specific index ETFs to take advantage of trends or opportunities in particular sectors.

For instance, if you think the tech sector is set for growth, you might invest in a tech-specific index ETF. The key here is to keep your finger on the pulse of market trends and adjust your investments accordingly.

Remember, though, that this approach can increase your risk, as you're putting all your eggs in one sector's basket. Make sure you're comfortable with the potential for rough waters ahead!

The Diversified Dolphin

Like its namesake, the diversified dolphin strategy is all about agility and adaptability. This approach involves investing in a mix of different index ETFs to diversify your portfolio across various market segments.

You might include broad market ETFs, sector-specific ETFs, and international ETFs in your mix, creating a balanced portfolio that can ride out different market conditions.

It's like being a dolphin, able to leap out of the water when the waves get rough and dive deep when there's opportunity below the surface.

Whether you're a blue whale, a shark, a dolphin, or some other kind of investment sea creature, remember that the key to successful investing is understanding your goals, knowing your risk tolerance, and staying consistent with your strategy.

Chapter 4: Sector and Thematic ETFs

4.1 Overview of Sector ETFs: Explanation of Sector ETFs

Sector ETFs: A Birds-eye View

So, what exactly are sector ETFs? Picture the broad market as a grand circus tent. This tent is divided into sections, or 'sectors', each housing a different act. You've got the clowns (let's say that's the tech sector), the acrobats (healthcare), the strongmen (industrials), the animal tamers (energy), and so on. Each act is its own spectacle, but together they make up the full circus performance.

Now, imagine you're an avid fan of the clowns and you want your investment to focus on them. You're not too concerned about the other acts. That's where sector ETFs come in. They allow you to invest specifically in the 'clown act', or in our real-world scenario, the tech sector.

Sector ETFs are funds that track specific sectors of the economy, like technology, healthcare, financials, energy, and so on. They invest in a basket of stocks belonging to companies operating within a specific sector, aiming to mirror the performance of that sector.

Selecting Your Sector

Sector ETFs allow you to capitalize on trends or growth in specific industries without having to select individual stocks. Think you have a crystal ball predicting the rise of renewable energy? A sector ETF lets you grasp the 'energy sector bar' and swing with it.

But remember, different sectors perform differently under varying market conditions. Some might be more volatile, some more steady. Some sectors might boom while others bust. Just like each circus act has its high and low points during a performance, each sector has its own performance cycle.

The Sizzle and the Steak

Sector ETFs can offer both potential sizzle (high returns if the sector is hot) and the steak (a steady, longer-term growth strategy if the sector is stable and predictable). For example, a hot, trendy sector like technology might be your 'sizzle', offering potential high returns but with higher risk. Meanwhile, a sector like consumer staples could be your 'steak', providing slower but steadier growth.

Remember, though, higher potential returns also mean higher potential risks. Swinging from a high bar might be exhilarating, but it also carries a higher risk of falling.

4.2 Thematic ETFs Explained: Description of Thematic ETFs and Current Popular Themes

Thematic ETFs: The Trend-Chasing Daredevils

Thematic ETFs are funds that focus on specific investment themes or trends. Rather than sticking to a particular sector or market capitalization, they cross sectors and sizes to invest in a collection of companies connected by a shared theme.

Think of it as buying a ticket to a specialty act at the circus. You're not there for the whole show; you're there for the stunt riders, the fire eaters, the sword swallowers – the ones that have caught the crowd's eye and are in the spotlight.

Rolling with the Times

The themes that these ETFs focus on can range from technological innovations like artificial intelligence, to social trends like clean energy, to demographic shifts like aging populations. They're a way to invest in emerging trends that could shape the future, capturing growth potential that might not be reflected in traditional sector classifications.

Popular Themes on the ETF Stage

As of our current date in mid-2023, here are a few of the hottest themes that are lighting up the ETF big top:

ESG (Environmental, Social, and Governance) Investing: These ETFs focus on companies that meet specific criteria in terms of their environmental impact, social responsibility, and governance practices. It's like investing in the circus acts that not only wow the crowd, but also treat their performers ethically, reduce their environmental footprint, and run a tight ship.

Clean Energy: As the world continues to shift away from fossil fuels, ETFs that focus on renewable energy and electric vehicles have been grabbing attention. These ETFs are like the high-flying aerialists of the circus, soaring above the ring as they harness the power of the wind and sun.

Artificial Intelligence and Robotics: The rapid advancement of AI and robotics technology has made this a hot theme in recent years. These ETFs are like the masterful magicians of the ETF circus, making impossible things happen right before our very eyes.

Healthcare Innovation: This theme focuses on companies driving breakthroughs in areas like biotechnology, genomics, and telemedicine. These ETFs are like the skilled acrobats, constantly pushing the boundaries of what's possible in the realm of health and medicine.

Thematic ETFs can add a dash of excitement to your portfolio, but remember that they also carry risks. They often focus on narrower, more volatile segments of the market, and their performance can hinge on the success of a particular trend. But for those willing to strap in and enjoy the ride, thematic ETFs can provide a unique way to access some of the most compelling stories unfolding on the financial stage. Now, hold onto your hats, folks, because next up we're diving into how to choose and invest in these daredevil performers!

4.3 Risks and Benefits: The High-Wire Balancing Act of Sector and Thematic ETFs

As with all investments, sector and thematic ETFs come with their own unique risks and benefits. Investing in them is a bit like performing a high-wire act in the ETF circus - a thrilling balancing act that requires careful consideration and a good sense of balance. Now, let's dissect these in detail, so you don't end up taking a financial tumble from the high-wire!

Benefits of Sector and Thematic ETFs

Targeted Exposure: These ETFs allow you to target specific sectors or trends, much like a circus performer focusing on a particular stunt to wow the crowd. This allows you to capitalize on growth or trends in a specific area without the need to research and invest in individual companies.

Diversification: Although they focus on a specific sector or theme, these ETFs are still diversified because they invest in a basket of companies. It's like having a safety net under your high-wire – if one company in the ETF takes a fall, your entire investment isn't wiped out.

Accessibility: Sector and thematic ETFs offer a straightforward way to access complex themes or industries. It's like having a VIP pass that gets you behind the scenes of the hottest acts in the investment circus, whether it's artificial intelligence, clean energy, or the booming tech sector.

Risks of Sector and Thematic ETFs

Concentration Risk: Because these ETFs focus on a particular sector or theme, they can be more susceptible to events or trends affecting that specific area. It's like walking the high-wire during a gusty wind – one strong gust (or sector downturn) could cause you to lose balance.

Volatility: Thematic ETFs, in particular, can be highly volatile. They often focus on emerging or disruptive trends, which can be unstable and uncertain. It's like adding flips and somersaults to your high-wire act – exciting, but risky!

Overfitting: Some themes can be narrow and overly specific, leading to a small selection of stocks that fit the criteria. This can lead to overfitting, where the ETF is over-exposed to a few specific companies. It's like walking the high-wire on stilts - one misstep from a key company, and your ETF could take a tumble.

While sector and thematic ETFs can play a valuable role in an investment portfolio, they should be used judiciously. Understanding the benefits and risks can help you maintain a balanced portfolio and stay upright on your investment high-wire. Up next, we'll be diving into some strategic tips for selecting and investing in sector and thematic ETFs. Don't let your guard down yet - the high-wire act isn't over!

4.4 Investment Strategies: The Art of Juggling Sector and Thematic ETFs in Your Portfolio

Investing in sector and thematic ETFs is like adding juggling to your ETF circus performance. Each ETF is a ball you have to keep in the air, and the success of your act depends on how well you can manage them all together. Let's break down some strategies to help you master the art.

Core-Satellite Approach

In this strategy, you structure your portfolio like a solar system. Your 'core' holdings (like broad market index ETFs) act as your sun—stable, reliable, and making up the bulk of your portfolio. Around this sun orbit your 'satellites'—smaller positions in sector or thematic ETFs that let you take advantage of specific trends or sectors.

In this approach, your core holdings aim to provide steady, long-term returns and diversification. The satellites, meanwhile, give you the chance to boost returns by capitalizing on hot trends or sectors.

This strategy can be a safer way to incorporate sector and thematic ETFs into your portfolio, as the core holdings can help cushion any blows if one of your sector or thematic 'balls' takes a dive.

Tactical Allocation

For those with a higher risk tolerance and a keen sense for market trends, a more active approach might be up your alley. In this strategy, you adjust your holdings in sector and thematic ETFs based on short-term market predictions or current economic conditions.

Picture this as a more complex juggling act, where you're swapping out balls mid-act based on the audience's reactions. It requires more skill and attention but can lead to higher returns if done successfully.

However, this approach comes with higher risk. Market predictions can be wrong, and if you bet on the wrong sector or theme, you could suffer losses. It's essential to balance this strategy with solid risk management practices.

Balancing Act

Whatever strategy you choose, remember that investing is a balancing act. Each sector or thematic ETF should have its role in your portfolio and contribute to your overall financial goals.

Consider your risk tolerance and investment horizon. Diversification is crucial to protect yourself from the potential pitfalls of a sector or thematic ETF that doesn't perform as expected.

Remember, the aim of your ETF circus act is not just to wow the audience with daring stunts, but to finish the performance in one piece and preferably richer in experience. Investing in sector and thematic ETFs can bring a dash of excitement to your act, but it should be done wisely and strategically. And with that, let's take a bow and prepare for our next act in the world of ETFs!

Chapter 5: Commodity and Bond ETFs

5.1 Introduction to Commodity ETFs: The Gritty Gladiators of the ETF Arena

Commodity ETFs! These funds are the gritty gladiators of the ETF arena, battling it out in the volatile world of commodities. Now, before we venture further into the gladiator pit, let's first equip ourselves with the basic knowledge about these robust warriors.

Commodity ETFs are exchange-traded funds that invest in physical commodities like agricultural goods, natural resources, and precious metals. Unlike your typical stock or bond ETF, commodity ETFs have the muscle to wrestle with tangible stuff – think gold, silver, oil, corn, wheat, and even livestock!

In the context of the ETF circus, if sector ETFs are the daring stunt riders, and thematic ETFs are the spellbinding magicians, then commodity ETFs are the strongmen, lifting and managing physical commodities in the investment showground.

There are two main types of commodity ETFs that investors can choose from:

Physical Commodity ETFs: These funds directly own a physical commodity and issue shares backed by these assets. The most common example is gold ETFs, which hold physical gold bars in a vault. Each share of the ETF represents a specific amount of gold. They're the weightlifters of the circus, showing off their shiny gold bars to the dazzled spectators.

Futures-Based Commodity ETFs: These ETFs don't hold the physical commodity; instead, they invest in futures contracts for a particular commodity. It's like betting on which strongman will lift the heaviest weight, rather than doing the heavy lifting yourself. However, these ETFs can be more complex and carry additional risks, as they're affected not just by the price of the commodity, but also by the shape of the futures curve.

5.2 Bond ETFs Explained: Understanding the Tightrope Walkers of the ETF Circus

Bond ETFs are exchange-traded funds that invest primarily in bonds. They could be likened to the tightrope walkers of our circus, who maintain their balance high above the ground. Instead of a balancing pole, they use diversification across many different bonds to help maintain stability.

Understanding the Balancing Act

Here's how it works. Bond ETFs hold a portfolio of bonds and aim to replicate the performance of a specific bond index. This could include government bonds, corporate bonds, municipal bonds, high-yield bonds, or other subsets of the bond market. Each unit you purchase in a bond ETF represents a stake in all those underlying bonds, so it's like having a diversified spot on the tightrope—giving you a better balance!

The primary return from a bond ETF comes from the interest payments, or coupon, generated by the bonds in the fund. These are typically distributed to the ETF holders on a regular basis, creating a steady stream of income much like the steady steps of a tightrope walker.

Navigating the Risks

However, don't be fooled into thinking this walk is a cakewalk. Bond ETFs also come with their set of risks, similar to the wind gusts and shakes that can destabilize even the most skilled tightrope walker. The main risks include interest rate risk, credit risk, and liquidity risk.

Interest Rate Risk: When interest rates rise, bond prices fall, and vice versa. So, if you're in a bond ETF when interest rates rise, the value of your ETF could fall.

Credit Risk: This is the risk that the bond issuer will default and not make the promised interest payments or return the principal upon maturity.

Liquidity Risk: Some bonds can be harder to buy or sell, which could impact the ETF's performance.

Just like how a tightrope walker would come prepared with a safety net, as an investor, you should also ensure you understand these risks and have strategies in place to manage them.

Now that we've untangled the complex rope of bond ETFs, let's continue our exploration. Next, we'll take a closer look at how to incorporate these cautious performers into your investment circus!

5.3 Risks and Returns: Evaluating the Highs and Lows of Commodity and Bond ETFs

Commodity ETFs: The Strongman's Highs and Lows

Returns: The potential returns from commodity ETFs can be impressive. They offer a golden opportunity to profit from price movements in commodities without needing to store barrels of oil or sacks of grain in your garage. When supply is scarce, and demand is high, commodity prices soar, and these ETFs can yield handsome returns.

Risks: However, the risks are as hefty as the weights our strongman lifts. Commodity ETFs are extremely sensitive to changes in supply and demand. Global economic conditions, geopolitical tensions, weather patterns, and even currency fluctuations can create price volatility. Also, futures-based commodity ETFs are prone to "contango" - a situation where the futures price of a commodity is above the expected spot price, which can erode returns over time.

Bond ETFs: Balancing on the Risk-Return Tightrope

Returns: Bond ETFs generate returns primarily from the interest income of the underlying bonds, which are distributed to investors periodically. Plus, if the bonds in the fund are sold at a higher price than they were bought, the ETF can generate capital gains. With various types of bond ETFs available, investors can choose from riskier high-yield bonds with higher interest payments to safer government bonds with lower returns.

Risks: On the flip side, bond ETFs can lose value if interest rates rise and bond prices drop. This is a particular concern for longer-term bonds, which are more sensitive to interest rate changes. Credit risk is another concern. If a bond issuer defaults, it could impact the ETF's value. Lastly, there's liquidity risk. If the bond market experiences a sudden drop in liquidity, it might be harder for the ETF to buy or sell bonds, which can impact its performance.

In the final analysis, it's all about finding the right performers for your investment show. Commodity and Bond ETFs, like all ETFs, have their own unique strengths and weaknesses. The trick is understanding these and finding the ones that align best with your financial goals and risk tolerance. So, as we conclude this act, ponder these insights and prepare yourself for the next exciting performance in the ETF circus!

5.4 Portfolio Diversification: Mastering the ETF Circus Act with Commodity and Bond ETFs

Now that we've peeked behind the curtain at the act put up by our commodity and bond ETF performers, it's time to learn how to direct them in the grand ETF circus show. Portfolio diversification is the name of this act, and our performers are all set to take the stage.

Adding Strength to Your Act with Commodity ETFs

Commodity ETFs are the strongmen of your portfolio, flexing their biceps when the equity markets may be underperforming. As commodities often have a low correlation with stocks and bonds, they can act as a valuable hedge against inflation and market volatility. In other words, when your acrobats and jugglers are tumbling, your strongman can hold up the fort!

Adding a touch of gold or a sprinkle of oil to your investment show through commodity ETFs can bring a new level of excitement and potential returns. However, remember that our strongman has a tendency to go overboard with his strength. Overexposure to commodities can make your portfolio volatile, so add just enough to bring diversity without tipping the scale.

Balancing Your Performance with Bond ETFs

Bond ETFs, our tightrope walkers, bring stability and predictability to your ETF circus. They generate regular income and can balance out the riskier parts of your portfolio. When your strongman is flexing too hard or your stunt riders are racing too fast, your tightrope walkers keep their balance, adding stability to your overall performance.

Their performance isn't affected as directly by market ups and downs as equity ETFs. So, even when your other performers may be taking a breather, your bond ETFs can keep the show going.

Mastering Your Circus Act

While our performers each bring something unique to the show, the trick is to find a balance that suits your audience – in this case, your financial goals and risk tolerance. As the ringmaster, you need to skillfully manage your performers, introducing new acts when needed and guiding the existing ones to adapt to the changing environment.

Diversifying with commodity and bond ETFs can help you create a show that's not just entertaining but also resilient. So, if the stock market sends in the clowns, your ETF circus is prepared to handle it with grace and strength. And with that, it's time to let the curtain fall on this chapter. Rest assured, the ETF circus has many more acts to unveil!

Chapter 6: ETF Trading Strategies

6.1 Buy and Hold: The Turtle Race of ETF Investing

We've seen high-flying acrobats, muscle-bound strongmen, and tightrope walkers in the ETF circus. But now, let's meet a different kind of performer – the turtle. Yes, a turtle! Why? Because the next strategy we're going to discuss is the ETF equivalent of a turtle race – the 'Buy and Hold' strategy.

No flipping, no daring leaps, no high-wire acts, just a steady, slow, and patient move towards the finish line. Doesn't sound as exciting as our other performers? Well, don't be so quick to judge. As Aesop's fable taught us, slow and steady can indeed win the race.

The Turtle's Creed: Buy and Hold

'Buy and Hold' is an investment strategy where you purchase an ETF and hold onto it for a long period, irrespective of market fluctuations. It's like our turtle steadfastly moving towards the finish line, unperturbed by what the hares around it are doing.

This strategy is grounded in the belief that in the long run, investment values will increase despite short-term market ups and downs. It's about committing to the journey, taking in the scenery, and not getting swayed by the speed demons racing by.

Benefits of Being a Turtle

Simplicity: Unlike active trading strategies that require frequent trades and constant monitoring of the market, the 'Buy and Hold' approach is simple. You buy an ETF and sit tight. It's as uncomplicated as the turtle's plodding pace.

Lower Costs: Each trade you make comes with transaction costs. The fewer trades you make, the lower your costs. Also, some tax advantages come with holding onto investments longer. Our turtle isn't just slow; it's smart!

Time in the Market: With 'Buy and Hold,' the focus is on 'time in the market' rather than 'timing the market.' History shows that markets tend to go up in the long run. By staying in the race longer, you're more likely to see your investments grow.

The Turtle's Caution

However, being a turtle also requires patience, discipline, and a thick shell to weather market downturns. There's also the risk of holding onto underperforming ETFs for too long, hoping for a turnaround. It's critical to review your portfolio regularly and make sure your investments are still in line with your financial goals.

So, if you're the kind of investor who prefers a steady pace, lower costs, and doesn't want to monitor market movements constantly, the 'Buy and Hold' strategy might suit you well. Like our turtle, you may not be the fastest, but you could still cross the finish line with a healthy portfolio in tow!

6.2 Swing Trading: The ETF Pendulum Play

After taking a cue from the slow and steady pace of the buy and hold strategy, let's crank up the tempo and step onto the dance floor of the ETF circus. This act is a thrilling blend of rhythm and precision, encapsulating the vivacious spirit of swing trading.

Swing trading, much like its jazz dance counterpart, involves quick movements – back and forth, up and down – as you attempt to capitalize on the ETFs' price 'swings' over a short period. It's like being the pendulum of a grand clock, swaying from one end to the other, capturing the rhythm of the ETF market.

The Swing Dance: How It Works

Swing trading revolves around capturing gains in an ETF's price within an overnight hold to several weeks. This strategy seeks to exploit the "swing" – the line of movement an ETF's price follows as it fluctuates.

Traders using this strategy will buy an ETF when they believe it is in an upward swing, sell it off when they believe that swing is nearing its peak, and then do the reverse for downward swings. The idea is to "buy the dip and sell the rip," as market mavens say.

Advantages of Dancing to the Swing

Shorter Holding Period: Unlike the 'Buy and Hold' strategy, swing trading involves a shorter holding period. This can limit exposure to risk from long-term market downturns and allow for faster profit realization.

Profit from Volatility: Market volatility is like the catchy beat of a swing dance. More volatility usually means more price swings, which can potentially lead to higher profits.

No Need for Constant Monitoring: Unlike day trading, swing trading does not require constant market monitoring. It's like having the time to enjoy the dance rather than constantly worrying about the next step.

The Swing Dancer's Word of Caution

Swing trading, like any complex dance move, does require practice and knowledge. Traders need to understand how to use technical analysis to identify price trends and potential swing points. It also demands discipline to stick to your predetermined entry and exit points and not get carried away by market noise.

Moreover, while swing trading may shield you from long-term volatility, it exposes you to short-term market risks. Plus, more frequent trading could mean higher transaction costs and taxes.

If you're someone who enjoys the adrenaline rush of rapid-fire trading without being glued to the market screen all day, swing trading could be your jam. It's a dance with the market pendulum, and if done right, you could step off the dance floor with some handsome profits!

6.3 Sector Rotation: The Carousel Ride of ETF Investing

As we've seen, the ETF circus is full of thrilling acts - the methodical turtle race of 'Buy and Hold,' the rhythmical dance of swing trading, and now, we're about to mount a merry-go-round. Yes, my friends, welcome to the ride known as 'Sector Rotation.' This strategy, just like a carousel ride, involves moving from one spot to another, or in this case, from one sector ETF to another, based on market cycles.

A Spin on the Carousel: How It Works

Sector Rotation is an investment strategy that involves moving investments among different sectors of the economy in an attempt to beat the market. The logic is that at any given time, certain sectors will outperform others. The trick is to spot which sector is on the upswing and jump on that horse before it gallops away. As the cycle shifts, you hop off and mount another steed that's ready to charge.

It's a strategy deeply rooted in the economic cycle, as different sectors tend to do better at different stages of the cycle. For instance, technology and consumer discretionary sectors often shine during an economic recovery, while utilities and consumer staples may be safer bets during a downturn.

Perks of Riding the Carousel

Capitalizing on Economic Cycles: The Sector Rotation strategy takes advantage of the cyclical nature of the economy. By predicting which sectors will perform best in each economic phase, you can potentially enhance your returns.

Diversification: Moving between different sector ETFs adds another layer of diversification to your portfolio. It's like enjoying all the different animals on the carousel, from the galloping horse to the soaring eagle.

Protection Against Downturns: By switching to defensive sectors during an economic downturn, this strategy can offer some level of protection against market volatility.

The Carousel Rider's Caution

Like any carousel ride, timing is crucial in Sector Rotation. Get on a horse too soon or too late, and you might miss the peak performance period. Moreover, predicting economic cycles with precision is no easy task; it requires a deep understanding of economic indicators and market trends.

More frequent trading can also mean higher transaction costs and taxes, and overexposure to a single sector can add sector-specific risks to your portfolio.

If you enjoy riding the waves of the economy and don't mind a bit of market forecasting, the Sector Rotation strategy could be your carousel ride in the ETF circus. Just remember, as with any merry-go-round, be prepared for a few spins before you hit your stride!

6.4 Leveraged and Inverse ETFs: The Daredevil Stunts of ETF Investing

So far, we've savored the slow-moving turtle race of 'Buy and Hold,' swayed to the rhythm of swing trading, and hopped onto the carousel of sector rotation. Now, it's time for the grand finale in our ETF circus: the daredevil stunts of leveraged and inverse ETFs.

Think of these as the trapeze artists and human cannonballs of the ETF world – high risk, high reward, and definitely not for the faint-hearted!

Trapeze Artists: Leveraged ETFs

Leveraged ETFs are designed to multiply the returns of a specific index or sector. For instance, a 2x leveraged ETF seeks to double the daily performance of its underlying index. Sounds fantastic, right? It's like swinging higher and higher on the trapeze, soaring above the ETF circus ring.

However, this also means that losses are multiplied. If the index falls by 1%, your 2x leveraged ETF will drop by 2%. If you can't stomach the thought of a swift plunge from the trapeze heights, this may not be your act.

Human Cannonballs: Inverse ETFs

Inverse ETFs, on the other hand, aim to achieve the opposite return of their benchmark index. They're used when investors expect a downturn and want to profit from it. It's like the thrill of the human cannonball act: you're betting on a spectacular fall (of the market) to send you soaring (in profits).

However, if the market goes up instead, your inverse ETFs will lose value. They're a high-stakes gamble that requires careful consideration and market knowledge.

The Daredevil's Words of Caution

Leveraged and inverse ETFs are complex financial instruments, and like all daredevil stunts, they come with significant risks. They're generally intended for short-term trading, as the compounding effect over a longer period can lead to results very different from the expected multiple of the index's return.

Furthermore, they require a solid understanding of the market and the mechanics of these ETFs. Also, frequent rebalancing can lead to higher transaction costs and tax implications.

Leveraged and inverse ETFs aren't for everyone. If you're an investor who loves the thrill of risk and has the knowledge to manage it, these ETFs can add some serious excitement to your investment portfolio. For others, it might be best to enjoy this act from the safety of the audience.

But remember, no matter what act you choose to perform in the ETF circus, always do so with a clear understanding of your financial goals, risk tolerance, and investment knowledge. The ultimate goal, after all, is not the thrill of the performance but the applause at the end – in the form of your investment success!

Chapter 7: Tax Considerations with ETFs

7.1 Basics of ETF Taxation: Making Sense of the Taxman's Rulebook

As we journey deeper into the labyrinth of the ETF universe, it's time we face an inevitable character - the taxman. Taxes might seem like the 'party pooper' at our ETF circus, but understanding their role is essential for any savvy investor.

Welcome, dear reader, to the Basics of ETF Taxation: where we decipher the taxman's rulebook, make sense of all those pesky regulations, and learn how to perform our financial maneuvers without tripping over tax hurdles.

Understanding the Tax Party: How ETFs are Taxed

Capital Gains Tax: This is the tax you pay when you sell an ETF for more than what you bought it for. It's like selling your circus ticket at a higher price. The difference in price is your 'capital gain,' and this gain is what gets taxed. The rate depends on whether it's a short-term (held for one year or less) or long-term (held for more than one year) capital gain, with short-term gains generally taxed at a higher rate.

Dividend Tax: Some ETFs, especially those that track indexes of income-generating assets like bonds or dividend-paying stocks, pay dividends to their shareholders. These dividends are taxed. The exact rate will depend on whether they are qualified or non-qualified dividends.

Interest Income Tax: For bond ETFs, the interest payments received are generally taxed as ordinary income. So if your ETF is a money-making magician pulling out interest income rabbits from its hat, the taxman is going to want a piece of the action.

Advantages of the Tax Big Top

You might be thinking, "Well, this tax thing seems like all pain and no gain!" But ETFs have a secret weapon up their sleeves. Due to their unique structure, they're often more tax-efficient than their mutual fund cousins. This efficiency is primarily due to the "in-kind" creation and redemption process of ETFs, which often allows them to avoid triggering capital gains.

The Taxman's Caution

Understanding ETF taxation isn't a walk in the park. It's more like a tightrope walk – it requires balance, precision, and a good dose of caution. Always remember, tax laws can be complex and vary from country to country, and this chapter offers a simplified overview.

For specific tax advice related to your circumstances, always consult a tax professional. It's like asking a seasoned circus performer for tips before attempting a tricky stunt.

So, roll up your sleeves and grab your calculators, as we delve deeper into the specifics of ETF taxation in the following sections. And remember, the goal is to juggle our ETF investments in a way that maximizes returns and minimizes tax headaches!

7.2 Qualified Dividends: The VIP Guests at the Tax Party

Now that we've acquainted ourselves with the three tax party guests – capital gains, dividend tax, and interest income tax – let's turn the spotlight onto a particular VIP guest: Qualified Dividends.

But what's so 'qualified' about them? Why do they get the red carpet treatment at the tax party? Well, put on your fancy hats and grab a glass of champagne, dear readers, as we pull back the velvet rope and welcome the 'qualified dividends.'

Rolling Out the Red Carpet: What are Qualified Dividends?

Qualified dividends are essentially the cream of the crop, the creme de la creme of dividends. They're the payments you receive from domestic or qualified foreign corporations that meet specific criteria set by the IRS.

And here's where the VIP status kicks in: these dividends are taxed at the same rates as long-term capital gains, which are generally lower than the rates for ordinary income.

Now, that's what I call a tax-efficient superstar!

The VIP List: Criteria for Qualified Dividends

So, how do you know if your dividends are mingling with the A-listers or hanging with the ordinary crowd? There are two primary conditions your dividends must meet to be 'qualified':

Holding Period: You must have held the ETF for more than 60 days during the 121-day period that begins 60 days before the ex-dividend date. In simpler terms, the taxman wants to see a little commitment before he rolls out the red carpet.

Qualified Corporation: The dividends must come from a U.S. corporation or a qualified foreign corporation. It's like an exclusive club membership – not everyone gets in.

An Affair to Remember: The Tax Implication

What does this VIP status mean for you, the investor? Well, it's all about the tax rates. Qualified dividends are taxed at rates of 0%, 15%, or 20%, depending on your taxable income and filing status. In contrast, non-qualified, or ordinary dividends, are taxed as regular income, and that rate could go up to 37%.

And, like any high-profile affair, the rules can get complex. For instance, certain types of income aren't eligible for qualified status, including dividends from REITs, master limited partnerships, and those received in retirement accounts, among others.

Understanding which of your dividends are 'qualified' can make a significant difference to your after-tax returns. But always remember: for detailed, personalized tax advice, nothing beats the counsel of a certified tax professional. After all, even VIPs need their advisors!

Here's to navigating the dazzling world of ETF dividends with style and tax efficiency. Cheers to the qualified dividends – the VIP guests that make the tax party a little more bearable!

7.3 Capital Gains: The High-Rollers of the ETF Tax Casino

Ready for a thrilling round at the ETF tax casino, where capital gains are the high-rollers betting on the rise and fall of your ETFs? Fasten your seatbelts, folks, because it's time to understand the risky, rewarding, and absolutely riveting world of capital gains taxes in relation to ETFs.

The High-Stakes Game: What are Capital Gains?

Picture this: you've bought an ETF at a certain price, let's call this the 'ante.' Then, after some time, you sell the ETF at a higher price - this is your 'winning hand.' The difference between your 'ante' and 'winning hand,' or in plain finance speak, your purchase and sale price, is your 'capital gain.'

If you've sold the ETF for less than what you bought it for, you've got a 'capital loss.' It's like losing a round at the high-stakes poker table.

The House Edge: *Short-Term vs. Long-Term Capital Gains*

Just like in any casino game, the house (or the taxman, in this case) has an edge. Capital gains are taxed, but the rate depends on whether it's a 'short-term' or 'long-term' capital gain.

Short-term Capital Gains: If you held your ETF for one year or less before selling, your gain is short-term. It's like a quick round of slots. These gains are taxed as ordinary income, which can range from 10% to 37%, depending on your tax bracket.

Long-term Capital Gains: If you held your ETF for more than a year before selling, your gain is long-term. It's like a strategic game of poker. These gains get a tax break and are taxed at 0%, 15%, or 20%, depending on your income level.

The Winning Strategy: Capital Loss Deductions

But what if you don't have a winning hand? What if you have a capital loss? Here's where the game gets interesting. You can use your capital losses to offset your capital gains, reducing your taxable income. If your losses exceed your gains, you can deduct the difference on your tax return, up to an annual limit of $3,000 (as of my knowledge cutoff in September 2021).

Play It Safe: The ETF Advantage

The casino of capital gains taxes can seem daunting, but here's a comforting fact: ETFs often have an advantage over mutual funds when it comes to generating fewer capital gains, thanks to the "in-kind" creation and redemption process. It means you're more likely to keep more of your winnings in your pocket.

Remember, understanding capital gains taxes can make a big difference in your ETF investment strategy. But when you're playing the high-stakes game, always have a tax professional by your side. They're like the experienced croupier who knows the ins and outs of the game.

Capital gains taxes: the exhilarating, essential, and ever-present aspect of your ETF investments. Now, go forth, play the game, and may the odds be ever in your favor!

7.4 International ETFs and Tax: The Globe-Trotter's Guide to Tax Navigation

Pack your bags and renew your financial passports, dear readers, because we're embarking on an international adventure! Yes, it's time to explore the vibrant, varied, and slightly vexing world of international ETFs and their tax implications.

Bon Voyage: What are International ETFs?

International ETFs offer a ticket to the investment world beyond your home country's borders. They track non-domestic indices or sectors, allowing you to invest in companies and markets across the globe. With these ETFs, you could own a slice of a German manufacturing company, a Korean tech giant, or an Australian mining corporation, all from the comfort of your home!

Customs Check: Tax on Dividends

When you're globetrotting with international ETFs, the first stop on the tax trail is usually dividends. These are taxed by both the foreign country and your home country.

Foreign Withholding Tax: Most countries tax dividends paid by their companies to foreign investors. This tax is typically withheld at the source, meaning the company paying the dividend deducts the tax before you receive it.

Home Country Tax: After the foreign tax, you'll face tax again in your home country. However, to prevent double taxation, many countries offer a foreign tax credit or deduction for the taxes already paid to the foreign country.

Border Control: Capital Gains Tax

Next up on our tax journey is the capital gains check. Luckily, the news here is typically good. In many cases, the sale of shares by a foreign investor isn't taxed by the foreign country. However, you'll likely owe capital gains tax in your home country, following the same short-term or long-term rules we covered earlier.

Navigating Tax Treaties

To ease the tax burden on international investors, many countries have tax treaties in place. These can lower the foreign withholding tax rate and help prevent double taxation. However, navigating tax treaties can be as complex as negotiating a maze in a foreign city without a map!

Layover: International Bond ETFs

For the brave investors venturing into the realm of international bond ETFs, brace for more complexity. The interest earned could face foreign withholding tax, and different tax treaty rules often apply compared to equity ETFs.

Travel Advisory: Seek Professional Help

International tax rules can change quickly and vary greatly between countries. Therefore, for specific, up-to-date advice, consult a tax professional familiar with international tax issues. They're like experienced travel guides, helping you navigate foreign terrain safely and efficiently.

And so, dear investors, armed with knowledge and caution, venture forth into the exciting world of international ETFs. Remember, as you traverse the global markets, keep a keen eye on your tax compass. Bon voyage and happy investing!

Chapter 8: Risk Management with ETFs

8.1 Understanding Risk: The Thrill-Seekers' Guide to ETF Investments

Fasten your safety harnesses and tighten your grip, dear investors, because we're embarking on the roller coaster ride that is ETF risk! Understanding risk in ETFs is akin to knowing when the loops, twists, and turns are coming. Let's dare to stare down the face of uncertainty and start identifying the risks associated with ETF investments.

Cliff Drop: Market Risk

The biggest drop in the roller coaster ride is often the scariest part. In ETF investing, that's the market risk. It's the risk that the entire market or sector your ETF is tracking will plummet. Like a roller coaster, the market has its ups and downs, but a sudden crash can make even the bravest thrill-seekers scream. Remember, diversification can help cushion the drop, but it can't entirely eliminate market risk.

Loop-the-Loop: Specific Risk

Specific risks are the surprising twists and turns of the roller coaster ride. These risks pertain to a specific company or industry in the ETF's portfolio. If a major company in the index faces scandal or bankruptcy, or if a whole industry is disrupted, your ETF could take a loop-the-loop tumble.

66

The Whip: Liquidity Risk

You know that moment when the roller coaster whips around a corner unexpectedly? That's liquidity risk. If an ETF doesn't have enough daily trading volume, you might not be able to buy or sell when you want to, or you may affect the price by doing so. And in times of market stress, even typically liquid ETFs can whip around and surprise you!

The Stuck Car: Counterparty Risk

Ever heard horror stories about a roller coaster car getting stuck? That's similar to counterparty risk in ETFs. This risk is especially pertinent to synthetic ETFs, where the counterparty (usually a bank) promises to pay the ETF the return of the index. If the counterparty defaults, your ETF ride could get abruptly stuck.

The Outdated Ride: Tracking Error

Imagine a roller coaster that promises a thrilling ride but turns out to be outdated and not as exciting. This disappointment is like the tracking error in ETFs. It's the risk that the ETF won't perfectly match the performance of the underlying index due to fees, trading costs, or other factors.

Remember, risk and return are two sides of the same coin in the thrilling theme park of investing. But with a firm grip on understanding the risks, you can better prepare for the ride and make sure it's a thrill, not a spill. Hold on tight, and enjoy the journey!

8.2 Diversification: The ETF Buffet of Risk Mitigation

Appetizer: Understanding Diversification

Diversification, in the investing world, is like not putting all your eggs in one basket or, in our buffet metaphor, not filling your plate with only one type of food. By spreading investments across different asset classes, sectors, and geographical areas, you reduce the risk of a poor performance in any one area significantly impacting your entire portfolio.

Main Course: Diversification with ETFs

ETFs make diversification as easy as scooping up your favorite dish at a buffet. Here's how:

Asset Class Diversification: ETFs cover a variety of asset classes, from stocks and bonds to commodities and real estate. It's like a well-stocked buffet offering everything from pasta to sushi, salads to roast meats.

Sector Diversification: Sector ETFs let you spread your risk across different industries. It's like diversifying between vegetarian, seafood, and meat dishes. If one sector experiences a downturn (say, technology), others (such as healthcare or utilities) may hold steady or even grow.

Geographical Diversification: International ETFs offer exposure to different economies worldwide. It's akin to choosing dishes from Italian, Mexican, Indian, or Chinese cuisine. This way, a downturn in one country or region doesn't empty your plate of returns.

Dessert: Diversification isn't Bulletproof

Like a buffet, diversification gives you plenty of choices, but it doesn't guarantee you'll love every dish or that every pick will be nutritious. Diversification can mitigate risk, but it can't eliminate it. Market risk, for instance, could cause nearly all stocks to drop simultaneously, no matter how well-diversified your ETFs are.

Digestif: Review and Rebalance

Just like you might revisit the buffet to balance your plate better, it's crucial to regularly review and rebalance your portfolio. As market values change, your asset allocation can shift away from your target. By rebalancing, you can ensure that your portfolio stays well-diversified and aligned with your risk tolerance and investment goals.

There you have it, the bountiful buffet of diversification made easy with ETFs. So go ahead, grab your plate, and start serving up a balanced meal of investments. Bon Appétit, or as we say in the investing world, Happy Diversifying!

8.3 Due Diligence: The Sherlock Holmes of ETF Investing

The Mystery: What is Due Diligence?

In the investing world, due diligence is your detective work. It's the careful examination and analysis you do before you buy an ETF, just like how Sherlock wouldn't accuse a suspect without investigating thoroughly first. By doing your due diligence, you unearth key clues about an ETF's structure, strategy, and potential risks.

Clue #1: Understanding the ETF Structure

Just as Holmes understood the structure of a crime scene, you should understand the structure of an ETF. Is it a physical ETF that holds the securities it tracks, or is it a synthetic ETF that uses derivatives to mimic an index? Each has its own set of risks and rewards.

Clue #2: Scrutinizing the Underlying Index

An ETF is only as good as the index it tracks, just like a detective is only as good as the clues they gather. When examining an ETF, scrutinize its underlying index. Is it broad-based, or does it track a specific sector or niche? Understanding this can help you grasp the ETF's potential performance and risk.

Clue #3: Examining the Expense Ratio

Every good detective knows money often plays a crucial role in any mystery. The same goes for ETFs. Check the ETF's expense ratio – the annual fee that all funds or ETFs charge their shareholders. A high expense ratio can significantly erode your returns over time, especially for long-term investments.

Clue #4: Checking the ETF's Liquidity

In the investment world, liquidity is a valuable commodity, much like a rare jewel in a mystery. Before investing, check the average trading volume of the ETF. An ETF with low liquidity can be harder to sell, and price swings can be more extreme.

Clue #5: Researching the ETF Provider

Finally, no investigation is complete without examining the characters involved. Look into the ETF provider's reputation and track record. A well-established provider is less likely to close an ETF, which can be a messy process for investors.

By approaching due diligence like a detective, you can make informed decisions and solve the mystery of successful ETF investing. Remember, as Sherlock Holmes once said, "It is a capital mistake to theorize before one has data." So gather your clues, do your detective work, and may the data always be with you!

8.4 Risk-Reward Ratio: The Thrilling Tightrope Walk of ETF Investing

Balancing Act 101: Understanding the Risk-Reward Ratio

The risk-reward ratio is the scale on which the potential profit (reward) of an investment is weighed against the potential loss (risk). Think of it as the tightrope walker's pole, helping to maintain balance. If one side gets too heavy, the act becomes dangerous.

For instance, if an ETF offers a chance to double your money but carries a risk of losing 75% of it, the risk-reward ratio is 0.75 to 1, which is not very favorable. On the other hand, if an ETF provides an opportunity to gain 20% with a potential 5% loss, the risk-reward ratio is 0.25 to 1, a more balanced proposition.

The Height of the Rope: Assessing Risk

The first step in this tightrope walk is gauging how high the rope is off the ground—figuring out the risk. Check the ETF's volatility, sector or market exposure, and underlying assets. Are you investing in a high-risk sector, or is the ETF based on a volatile foreign market? Is the ETF thinly traded, creating liquidity risk? Understand these risks before you step onto the tightrope.

The Length of the Pole: Calculating Reward

Next, consider the length of your balance pole—potential rewards. Check the ETF's past performance, its dividend yield, and the growth potential of its sector or market. Remember, past performance isn't indicative of future results, but it can help gauge the ETF's potential.

The Art of Balance: Making the Decision

Now comes the actual balancing act. Compare the potential risks with the potential rewards. Is the risk-reward ratio balanced in favor of reward, or are you teetering dangerously towards the risk? Always aim for an ETF where the potential reward outweighs the risk, without the difference being so significant that it unsettles your overall portfolio balance.

The Safety Net: Diversification

Even the most skilled tightrope walkers have safety nets. In ETF investing, that's diversification. It helps ensure that if one ETF fails, others in your portfolio can still succeed, cushioning any fall.

Remember, investing is not about avoiding risks but understanding them. By calculating the risk-reward ratio, you can confidently walk the investing tightrope. After all, what's life without a little thrill, a little risk, and a whole lot of balance! So, ready to step onto the ETF tightrope? Keep the balance, and enjoy the view!

Chapter 9: Building an ETF Portfolio

9.1 Portfolio Construction: Building Your ETF Dream House

Foundation: Investment Goals and Risk Tolerance

Before we bring in the bulldozers, we need to lay a solid foundation. This starts with identifying your investment goals. Are you saving for a dream vacation, preparing for retirement, or building a nest egg for unforeseen circumstances?

Next, you must understand your risk tolerance. This depends on your financial situation, investment timeline, and how much volatility you can stomach. A younger investor may have a higher risk tolerance and a long-term perspective, allowing for more aggressive growth ETFs. In contrast, a retiree might want to preserve capital, leaning towards income-focused or bond ETFs.

Framework: Asset Allocation

Now that we have a strong foundation, let's build the framework, otherwise known as asset allocation. This is the mix of asset classes in your portfolio, like equities (stocks), fixed income (bonds), commodities, and real estate.

Consider your investment goals and risk tolerance when choosing your asset mix. A common rule of thumb is the "120 minus your age" rule, which suggests that the percentage of your portfolio invested in stocks should be approximately 120 minus your age, with the remainder in bonds. For example, a 30-year-old would have roughly 90% in stocks and 10% in bonds.

Remember, the goal here is to create a portfolio diverse enough to weather market fluctuations without causing sleepless nights.

Floors: Diversifying with ETFs

Now, let's add the floors to our building, which represent different sectors, industries, or regions. Here's where ETFs shine! With ETFs, you can easily achieve diversification across different areas without the need to research and buy individual stocks.

You might have a floor (ETF) dedicated to technology, another for healthcare, another for international markets, and so forth. This way, a slump in one sector won't collapse your whole building.

Interiors: Choosing the Right ETFs

The interiors of your house make it unique and cater to your specific needs. Similarly, the choice of ETFs in your portfolio should reflect your investment style and objectives.

Consider factors like the ETF's expense ratio, its underlying index, liquidity, and the ETF provider's reputation. Don't forget to look at the ETF's holdings to make sure it fits your intended sector, industry, or region.

Maintenance: Regular Reviews and Rebalancing

Just like a house needs regular maintenance, your portfolio does too. Over time, as some ETFs perform better than others, your asset allocation might get out of balance.

Regularly review and rebalance your portfolio to ensure it stays aligned with your goals and risk tolerance.

And there we have it—your ETF portfolio, standing tall and strong like your dream house. Just remember, Rome wasn't built in a day, and neither will your portfolio be. It takes time, patience, and a bit of elbow grease. But when it's done, you'll have a financial fortress that can weather the storms and sunshine of the market. Happy building!

9.2 Strategic Asset Allocation: The Financial GPS for your ETF Journey

The Map: What is Strategic Asset Allocation?

Strategic asset allocation (SAA) is your financial GPS, guiding you through the investment journey. It's a portfolio strategy that sets targets for different asset classes and rebalances the portfolio back to these targets as needed.

Imagine you're planning a road trip. You decide beforehand how much time you'll spend on the highway (stocks), small country roads (bonds), dirt trails (commodities), and in various cities (sectors). That's your SAA.

The aim is to strike a balance that matches your long-term financial goals and risk tolerance. The targets usually remain unchanged unless there's a significant shift in your life, like a new job, retirement, or winning a lottery (fingers crossed!).

Fueling Up: Building Your Asset Allocation

First things first, let's fuel up! In investing terms, this means setting your asset allocation. Based on your risk tolerance and investment goals, decide what percentage of your portfolio you want in different asset classes. For example, you might allocate 60% to stocks, 30% to bonds, and 10% to commodities.

The Journey: Diversification with ETFs

Now we hit the road! In this step, you select ETFs that represent the different asset classes and sectors. Remember, it's crucial to diversify your ETFs across various sectors and regions. ETFs are perfect for this as they provide exposure to a wide range of assets without needing to buy each individually. So buckle up, and enjoy the scenic diversification route!

Detours: Market Fluctuations

Like any good road trip, you'll face detours along the way in the form of market fluctuations. Say the stock market has a great year, and your stock ETFs now make up 70% of your portfolio, instead of the 60% target. It's time to recalculate your route!

Re-routing: Rebalancing Your Portfolio

When your portfolio strays from the planned route, it's time to rebalance. In our detour example, you'd sell some stock ETFs and buy more bonds and commodities to bring your portfolio back to the 60/30/10 allocation. This maintains the risk-reward ratio that you initially set and keeps you on track to your financial destination.

Arriving: Achieving Your Financial Goals

With the GPS of SAA, you can navigate the investment journey, survive the detours, and finally arrive at your financial goals. But remember, this journey is a marathon, not a sprint. It takes time, patience, and a commitment to the route you've set.

9.3 Rebalancing Your Portfolio: The Art of Financial Feng Shui

The What: Defining Portfolio Rebalancing

In the interior design world of investing, portfolio rebalancing is the process of realigning the proportions of your assets to maintain your desired asset allocation. It's like moving your furniture around when things feel "off" in your living room.

Say you started with a 70/30 stock/bond split in your portfolio. After a year of booming equities, your portfolio drifts to an 80/20 split. It's time to sell some stocks and buy some bonds to return to the original 70/30 blueprint.

The Why: Benefits of Rebalancing

Rebalancing has three main perks:

Risk Control: Just like you wouldn't put all your furniture on one side of the room, you don't want all your money in one asset class. Rebalancing prevents your portfolio from leaning too heavily towards high-performing (and potentially high-risk) assets.

Maintain Strategy: Your original asset allocation is your game plan. It reflects your risk tolerance and financial goals. Rebalancing ensures you stick to the plan, even when the market lures you with dazzling returns.

Buy Low, Sell High: If an asset class is performing well, you're selling it when its price is high. If another is underperforming, you're buying it when its price is low. In other words, rebalancing naturally follows the golden rule of investing: buy low, sell high.

The How: Rebalancing Strategies

There are two common ways to rebalance:

Calendar Rebalancing: This is the annual spring cleaning of portfolio rebalancing. You set a specific time, usually every quarter, semi-annually, or annually, to check if your portfolio needs a tidy-up.

Threshold Rebalancing: In this method, you set specific boundaries for your asset allocation. If any asset class drifts away from its target by a pre-determined percentage (say, 5 or 10 percent), it triggers a rebalance.

The When: Timing for Rebalancing

Rebalancing does involve transaction costs and potential tax consequences, so it's not something you want to do every day. Most experts suggest rebalancing at least once a year, but it also depends on market conditions, transaction costs, and your personal comfort level.

The art of rebalancing your portfolio! Just remember, maintaining balance is key to achieving harmony, whether it's in your living room or your ETF portfolio. Now, who's ready for some financial Feng Shui?

9.4 Evaluating Performance: The Annual Report Card for Your ETF Portfolio

It's time for the report card of your financial offspring – your ETF portfolio. And just like proud parents at a school open-house, you'll want to understand how your portfolio has been performing. So put on your reading glasses and get your red pen ready, because we're going to evaluate the performance of your ETF portfolio!

The Metrics: Performance Indicators

Evaluating a portfolio isn't as simple as checking the grades on a report card; it's a multi-faceted process that involves several metrics:

Absolute Returns: This is the most straightforward measure—how much has your portfolio grown or shrunk? It's important, but remember that context matters. If the broader market is up 15% and your portfolio is only up 5%, you're underperforming despite the growth.

Relative Returns: Here's where we bring in that context. Compare your portfolio's performance to a benchmark index. This can help you see how your ETFs are doing compared to the overall market or specific sectors.

Risk-Adjusted Returns: This is like grading on a curve. Sure, your portfolio might have had high returns, but if it took a roller-coaster of risk to get there, it may not be as impressive. Metrics like the Sharpe Ratio can help you understand how much return you're getting for each unit of risk taken.

Portfolio Diversification: How well is your portfolio diversified across different asset classes and sectors? A well-diversified portfolio helps to manage risk.

The Approach: Top-Down and Bottom-Up Analysis

For a holistic view of your portfolio's performance, it's good to use a mix of top-down and bottom-up analysis.

In **Top-Down Analysis**, you start with the big picture: how is the economy doing? What are the market trends? Then you drill down to sectors, then to specific ETFs. This helps you understand how external factors are impacting your portfolio.

In **Bottom-Up Analysis**, you start with your individual ETFs. How are they performing? What's driving their performance? Then you look at the sectors they're in, and finally at the broader market. This helps you understand how your specific investments are driving your portfolio's performance.

The Frequency: Timing Your Evaluations

The frequency of portfolio evaluation depends on your investing style. Active traders might do it daily or weekly, but for most long-term investors, a quarterly or semi-annual review is usually sufficient.

Chapter 10: The Future of ETFs

10.1 Trends in the ETF Market: Navigating the Financial Zeitgeist

We're about to jet off into the future to explore the current trends and developments in the ever-evolving ETF market.

Trend 1: Thematic ETFs

Whoever said "don't mix business with pleasure" clearly didn't foresee the rise of thematic ETFs. From clean energy to e-sports, thematic ETFs allow investors to align their portfolios with their passions, values, or convictions about future trends. They're the portfolio equivalent of having your cake and eating it too. Yum!

Trend 2: ESG Investing

ESG investing stands for Environmental, Social, and Governance, and it's the investment world's equivalent of being a good citizen. More investors want their money to support sustainable practices, and ETF issuers are answering the call. ESG ETFs are growing faster than bamboo on steroids, so expect to see more on the horizon!

Trend 3: Active ETFs

Hold onto your hats, folks. Actively managed ETFs are shaking up the traditionally passive world of ETF investing. These funds have managers making strategic decisions in an attempt to outperform a benchmark index, merging the accessibility of ETFs with the potential of active management. It's like having a gourmet chef in your fast-food joint!

Trend 4: Cryptocurrency ETFs

Cryptocurrency ETFs are as trendy as avocado toast in a hipster café. As digital currencies like Bitcoin and Ethereum become more mainstream, these ETFs offer investors a way to get exposure to crypto without having to figure out how to store a digital wallet. However, regulatory hurdles are as plentiful as potholes on a city street, so tread carefully.

Trend 5: Innovation-Focused ETFs

Lastly, we have ETFs that focus on innovative technologies. Whether it's artificial intelligence, electric vehicles, genomics, or fintech, these ETFs aim to provide exposure to cutting-edge companies. It's a bit like investing in the Jetsons!

10.2 Innovations in ETFs: Welcome to the ETF Innovation Lab!

Innovation 1: Non-Transparent ETFs

First, in our tour, we have non-transparent ETFs, the James Bonds of the ETF world. These ETFs allow active managers to hide their secret sauce (i.e., their portfolio holdings) from the prying eyes of the public. Now, that's innovation with a cloak of invisibility!

Innovation 2: Synthetic ETFs

Next up, we have synthetic ETFs. These don't hold the actual assets they're supposed to track. Instead, they use derivatives and swaps to mimic the performance of an index. It's like having a robot butler – not quite the real thing, but it can get the job done!

Innovation 3: ETFs of ETFs

In the spirit of Russian nesting dolls, we present you with ETFs of ETFs. These funds don't invest directly in stocks or bonds but in other ETFs! This allows for a built-in diversification strategy and offers exposure to a wide array of assets with a single purchase.

Innovation 4: Buffer ETFs

Buffer ETFs are the ETF market's answer to the volatility vultures. These funds offer protection (a buffer) against a certain percentage of losses in return for capping gains during a specified time period. It's like an airbag for your investments!

Innovation 5: Quantum Computing and AI-Driven ETFs

Finally, we've got ETFs that use artificial intelligence and quantum computing to pick stocks. By analyzing vast amounts of data at lightning speed, these ETFs attempt to make optimal investment decisions. It's like having a supercomputer as your financial advisor!

The latest and greatest from the ETF Innovation Lab. But remember, while innovation is exciting, it also brings new risks and complexities. Always do your research and consider your risk tolerance before you invest in the next big thing. Until next time, stay curious, my innovative investors!

10.3 Regulatory Considerations: The ETF Regulatory Rollercoaster

Regulatory Consideration 1: The SEC's Rule 6c-11

In the spirit of streamlining and modernizing the ETF industry, the SEC passed Rule 6c-11 in September 2019, which brought some sighs of relief. The rule allows ETFs to operate without obtaining an exemptive order, saving time and money. But like all thrilling rides, it came with a twist. ETFs are now required to provide daily disclosures on their websites about their portfolios. So, in essence, transparency got a bit of a boost!

Regulatory Consideration 2: Non-Transparent ETFs

Speaking of transparency, the world of non-transparent ETFs (also known as "black box ETFs") has regulators in a bit of a tizzy. While they allow fund managers to keep their strategies close to their chests, regulators are still grappling with how to balance innovation and investor protection. Will these mysterious funds change the game or just complicate it? Only time will tell!

Regulatory Consideration 3: Cryptocurrency ETFs

Next up, we have the crypto cliffhanger. Regulatory approval for cryptocurrency ETFs has been as elusive as a unicorn. While some countries have given the green light, others, including the U.S., are proceeding with caution due to concerns about volatility, manipulation, and custody issues. Crypto ETFs are on the brink, waiting for regulatory barriers to crumble. Hold onto your hats!

Regulatory Consideration 4: ESG Reporting Standards

Finally, we have the swirling vortex of ESG (Environmental, Social, and Governance) reporting standards. As ESG investing gains traction, regulators are considering whether mandatory, standardized reporting should be required to ensure investors aren't being "greenwashed" by false or misleading claims. How this plays out could significantly impact ESG ETFs.

10.4 Preparing for the Future: Your ETF Time Machine Awaits

Tip 1: Lifelong Learning

Remember when you thought you'd never need to learn anything after graduating? Ah, such youthful naivety! Lifelong learning is crucial in the ever-changing financial landscape. Staying abreast of industry news, attending webinars, reading financial literature, and keeping up with regulatory changes will ensure you're always in the know. Remember, knowledge is power (and also potentially profits)!

Tip 2: Diversify, Diversify, Diversify

The world of ETFs offers numerous opportunities for diversification – from sector to geographic to thematic. As the market evolves, don't forget the golden rule of not putting all your eggs in one basket. Embrace the variety, and remember that your risk tolerance and investment goals should guide your diversification strategy.

Tip 3: Embrace Technology

Technology isn't just for those tech ETFs. It's a powerful tool for investors too. From financial news apps to robo-advisors, technology can help you track market trends, manage your portfolio, and make informed decisions. So, don't be a digital dinosaur. Get tech-savvy!

Tip 4: Stay Calm and Carry On

Change can be scary, but remember to stay calm and carry on. Volatility is part and parcel of investing, and the ETF landscape will continue to evolve. Don't panic when you hear about market fluctuations or regulatory changes. Instead, take a deep breath, do your research, and consider how these changes fit into your long-term investment strategy.

Tip 5: Seek Professional Advice

As we sail into the future, don't forget you're not alone on this journey. A trustworthy financial advisor can provide valuable insights, help you understand complex developments, and guide your decision-making process. Sometimes, it pays to have a seasoned co-pilot!

Chapter 11: Maximizing ETFs in Your Investment Journey

11.1 Recap: ETFs for Diversification and Growth: A Walk Down ETF Memory Lane

Remember back in the early chapters when we first introduced ETFs? Ah, such innocent times. We discussed the ETFs' versatility, their potential for lower costs, and of course, their ability to offer you a slice of multiple pies in a single bite! Yes, diversification is one of the major attractions of ETFs.

As we moved further down the lane, we encountered the various inhabitants of the ETF world. From the common Index ETFs, the industrious Sector and Thematic ETFs, to the steady Bond ETFs and the adventurous Commodity ETFs, each one provided a unique way to spread your investments across different asset classes, industries, or even countries.

And who can forget the thrilling world of ETF trading strategies? The patient Buy and Hold strategy, the agile Swing Trading, and the ever-circling Sector Rotation strategy, all geared towards nurturing growth in your portfolio. Of course, the adrenaline junkies amongst us will also recall the thrilling, albeit risky, world of Leveraged and Inverse ETFs.

The ETF landscape is a vast and varied one, offering numerous opportunities for diversification and growth. Whether you're a newbie investor dipping your toes in the investment pool or a seasoned veteran looking to spruce up your portfolio, ETFs could be the trusty tool you need. So, strap on your financial tool belt, and let's prepare for the final chapter of our ETF journey!

11.2 Building Confidence as an ETF Investor: Becoming an ETF Superhero

Tool 1: Knowledge is Power

Remember our good friend lifelong learning from Chapter 10? Well, he's back! The first tool in your kit is knowledge. Keep expanding your understanding of the ETF world – from financial news outlets, financial education websites, to financial literature (like this fabulous book you're reading!). The more you know, the more confident you'll feel making investment decisions.

Tool 2: Practical Experience

There's nothing like rolling up your sleeves and getting your hands dirty. Begin with virtual trading platforms or paper trading to simulate real ETF trading without actual monetary risk. The experience can help you understand how different ETFs behave under various market conditions and enhance your decision-making skills.

Tool 3: A Solid Plan

What's a superhero without a plan? Developing a well-researched investment strategy and sticking to it is a crucial part of becoming confident in your ETF investing journey. Remember to factor in your investment goals, risk tolerance, and time horizon when crafting your plan.

Tool 4: Professional Guidance

Even superheroes have sidekicks! A trustworthy financial advisor can act as your investing sidekick, providing you with valuable advice, helping you understand complex market scenarios, and steering you through the highs and lows of the ETF landscape.

Tool 5: Emotional Resilience

Last but not least, an often-underrated tool - emotional resilience. Investing can be a rollercoaster ride, and the ability to stay calm during market volatility is an invaluable asset.

The path to confidence in ETF investing involves a mix of knowledge, experience, planning, professional guidance, and emotional resilience. It's time to grab your toolkit and start building the confidence you need to navigate the world of ETFs successfully. To infinity and beyond!

11.3 Lifelong Learning and Adaptation: Becoming an Investing Chameleon

We're nearing the end of our ETF journey, but the real adventure is just beginning. The key to a successful investing career lies in a couple of deceptively simple concepts: lifelong learning and adaptability. Let's unwrap these ideas, shall we?

Lifelong Learning: Your Trusty GPS

In our ever-evolving financial world, with its constant flux of new developments, trends, and regulations, knowledge is more than just power – it's your GPS through the investment landscape. Lifelong learning ensures that your GPS stays updated, guiding you smoothly through the twists and turns of the ETF market.

A proactive approach to learning – attending webinars, reading up on market news, keeping up with this book's future editions (hint, hint) – ensures that you stay ahead of the curve. With your trusty GPS (aka lifelong learning), you'll navigate the ETF path with the confidence of an experienced explorer!

Adaptability: Your All-Terrain Vehicle

If lifelong learning is your GPS, then adaptability is your all-terrain vehicle, ready to tackle any road, no matter how rocky! The ETF landscape, like any financial market, is dynamic. It can shift faster than a chameleon changes its color.

Adaptability involves adjusting your investment strategies to respond to market trends or unexpected changes. Maybe it's reallocating your assets amid market volatility, or perhaps it's exploring new, innovative ETFs that align with future trends. The financial chameleon is always ready to adapt and thrive in changing environments.

11.4 Final Thoughts and Takeaways: The Grand ETF Finale

ETFs: Your Investment Swiss Army Knife: ETFs are a versatile financial instrument that offers an all-in-one solution to diversification, cost-effectiveness, and flexibility. Remember, whether you're a newbie investor or a seasoned veteran an ETF can be your trusty sidekick in the financial landscape.

Know Your ETFs: Like different tools in a toolbox, various types of ETFs serve different purposes. From index to sector, from commodity to bond ETFs, each type has its unique characteristics and role in your portfolio. Choose wisely, and remember, one size doesn't fit all.

Strategize like a Chess Master: Your approach to ETF investing should be like a well-thought-out chess game. Whether you choose the patient 'Buy and Hold' strategy, the agile 'Swing Trading' approach, or the ever-evolving 'Sector Rotation' tactic, make sure it aligns with your financial goals and risk tolerance.

Tax Considerations: An Investor's Homework: Taxes and investments go hand-in-hand. Being well-versed with the tax implications of ETFs - from qualified dividends to capital gains, can save you from unpleasant surprises during the tax season.

Future-Proofing: The Crystal Ball Gazing: Keeping up with the latest trends, innovations, and regulatory changes in the ETF space is crucial for future-proofing your investment strategies. Remember, lifelong learning and adaptability are your companions in this journey.

So, there you have it, my financial comrades. I hope you've found this journey through the world of ETFs enlightening and entertaining. As we part ways, remember that the road to financial freedom is a marathon, not a sprint. It's marked by continuous learning, prudent decisions, and a whole lot of resilience.

Here's to you, future ETF masters. May your portfolios be ever diverse, your decisions ever wise, and your financial future ever bright. Until our next adventure together, farewell!

11.5 The Journey Ahead: Grab Your Financial Compass and Let's Go!

Imagine your financial journey as an epic treasure hunt. You, intrepid explorer, are armed with a detailed map—your solid grasp of ETFs and financial strategies—and a reliable compass—your personal investment goals and risk tolerance. The treasure? A robust, diversified portfolio, and the peace of mind that financial security brings.

As you venture forth, remember, every step on your investment path is an opportunity to learn, grow, and refine your approach. Some days, you'll stride confidently down a sunlit path, your portfolio growing and your decisions paying off. Other days, you'll navigate tricky turns and unexpected market turbulence. But remember, even setbacks are invaluable chances to learn, adapt, and become a more resilient investor.

Lifelong learning isn't just a buzzword—it's your guidepost in this journey. Markets will evolve, new ETF products will emerge, regulations will change. Embrace the continuous cycle of learning, adjusting your strategies with the agility of a financial acrobat and the patience of a diligent scholar.

Don't be disheartened if your journey seems slow or arduous. True investing success doesn't happen overnight—it's the fruit of consistent effort, steady discipline, and well-calculated decisions. And always remember, it's about your personal financial goals and comfort with risk. Don't compare your journey with others—focus on your path, your progress.

And finally, take a moment now and then to appreciate how far you've come. From the fledgling investor who first opened this book to the savvy ETF navigator you've become—you've come a long way, my friend!

So, go forth, brave adventurer! Your journey beckons, filled with the thrill of investment victories, the wisdom from lessons learned, and the promise of financial growth. With your ETF knowledge, your personal financial compass, and a spirit of relentless curiosity, you're ready to conquer the exciting world of ETF investing. May your journey be fruitful, your learning unending, and your success resounding.

Onward to glory, dear reader! The journey is all yours.

Chapter 12: Closing: Your ETF Investment Journey - Time to Chart Your Course

Dear reader, we've traversed quite a long road together, haven't we? From the bustling beginnings of ETFs to the dynamic trends of their future, it has been an enlightening journey—one filled with laughter, a-ha moments, and plenty of playful metaphors. Now, we stand at the end of this road, with the wide expanse of your personal investment journey stretching out before us.

The lessons you've learned and the insights you've gathered from our escapades are now yours to own and apply. Consider them your personal toolbox for the road ahead—each piece of knowledge a tool designed to help you navigate your unique financial landscape.

With this treasure trove of wisdom in your grasp, you are prepared to carve your own path through the complex world of ETF investing. Just as a seasoned captain sails the vast ocean with confidence, may you too steer your investment ship with poise, no matter the market climate.

Always remember that investing is not a one-size-fits-all endeavor. Like a bespoke suit, your investment strategy should be tailored to fit your unique needs, risk tolerance, and financial goals. Whether you wish to accumulate wealth for retirement, save for a dream home, or support a child's education, may your ETF investment strategies serve as steadfast vehicles to get you to your financial destinations.

Looking ahead, we know that the world of ETFs is dynamic and ever-changing. As you journey onward, keep your eyes open and your mind curious. Staying informed about emerging trends, innovative ETF products, and changing regulations is not just an added advantage—it's a necessity in the vibrant landscape of ETF investing.

As our shared journey ends, yours is just beginning. It's time for you to set sail on the vast sea of investment opportunities. We may part ways here, but remember, the lessons, the laughter, and the wisdom from this book will always accompany you.

I hope this book has not only equipped you with knowledge but also ignited in you a passion for ETF investing—a spark that will illuminate your path as you journey forward.

So, step forward bravely into the exciting world of ETFs. You are now more than just a reader. You are an informed investor, ready to make smart, strategic decisions. As you embark on your journey, know that success lies not just in the destination but also in the journey itself.

Here's to you, the savvy investor—may your investments grow, your wisdom deepen, and your journey be filled with success and satisfaction. Until we meet again on the pages of another book, bon voyage, dear reader! Here's to the journey ahead and to the exciting world of ETFs—it's your world to conquer!